Perspective: Baltimore

KYLE POMPEY

Pompey, Kyle.
Perspective: Baltimore

ISBN-13: 978-0692970676 (Nice Shot Media) (Paperback Edition)

ISBN-10: 0692970673 (Paperback Edition)

Printed in the United States of America.

All Photography by Kyle Pompey.
Book design by www.nikiearedmond.com.
Edited by Kerry Graham.

Dennis Lewis.

"Do Great, Be Great, Legacy!"

Kyle Pompey

Dedicated to George Branson Raiford

"The realest one"

Freethought:

a philosophical viewpoint which holds that positions
regarding truth should be formed on the basis of logic,
reason, and empiricism, rather than authority, tradition,
revelation, or other dogma.

TABLE OF CONTENTS

The titles for the photos are intentionally missing.
As you write your perspectives of the photos, put your title of each one here.

PREFACE

Kyle "Nice Shot" Pompey is a gift to Baltimore, a legend.

Not because of his success, popularity or dreams--but his bravery. Pompey has been brave enough to be himself in a time when many people aimlessly follow others. You see, Kyle is from east Baltimore in a section of the city where photographers, sculptors, painters and visual artists in general didn't exist. Ball players had other athletes to look up to, just as dealers had street guys to follow, but it wasn't always like that for artists. And you couldn't just walk out into the street and say, "Yo I want to be the greatest photographer in the world!" Everyone would laugh at you, but thankfully, that didn't stop Kyle.

He ignored tradition, bought a camera and taught himself how to shoot. Starting out at parties and local functions to working his way up to celebrity fashion shoots, gallery exhibits and having his work displayed all over Baltimore and in many parts of the country, Kyle was the first professional photographer from the hood, at least in Baltimore. I'm sure there were other guys taking pictures, but no one that we knew, no one like Kyle.

A person with Kyle Pompey's talent and ambition could probably live anywhere in the world and yet he decides to stay in his hometown of Baltimore--inspiring the next generation of photographers, and being the type of leader who is more than capable of laying the foundation for what working Black artists should look like in Baltimore.

Young people from all over the city are photographers because of Kyle Pompey--not only do they follow his moves, they borrow his equipment, they use his studio, and learn from his guidance. Guidance that he can't wait to share, and that is what makes Kyle legendary-- his ability to lift as he climbs so that we all can win.

Pompey's first book, *Perspective: Baltimore,* will only add to this legacy. It will give people a chance to not only celebrate his amazing images, but also to define them from their own perspectives, create conversations and ultimately carve out their piece of Baltimore.

D. Watkins, Author
NEW YORK TIMES BEST SELLER

WHAT BALTIMORE DO YOU LIVE IN?

So my black friends call it Baldamore, Harm City, or Bodymore Murderland. My white friends call it Balti-mo, Charm City, or Smalltimore while falling in love with the quaint pubs, trendy cafés and distinctive little shops. I just call it home.

We all love Baltimore, Maryland. It's one of those places that people never leave–literally. I know people, blacks and whites, who have been residents for 30-plus years and haven't even been as north as Philly or as south as DC.

Baltimore is one of the few major metropolitan cities with a small-town feel. The town was founded in 1729 and named after the Englishman Cecilius Calvert, better known as Lord Baltimore. In the years that followed, Germans and Scots settled the cheap land, which was too poor for tobacco farming but good enough for wheat. Proximity to water helped Baltimore flourish, with a thriving ship market at Fell's Point, now a hip waterfront area.

Eventually, Baltimore took off in a major way, and as industry grew so did the need for slaves. By 1810 Baltimore had 4,672 slaves, mostly hired out by cash-strapped owners from upper Maryland. In the heyday of the antebellum South, before the Civil War, some of those Baltimore slaves made enough money on the side to buy their own freedom and eventually the freedom of their family and friends.

Maryland sided with the Union during the Civil War by not declaring secession, even though it was a slave state–though some people in southern Maryland joined the Confederates anyway to keep their slaves and their tobacco farms. Some Confederate supporters attacked Union soldiers, causing 12 deaths and the Baltimore riot of 1861. After that, the Union Army had to step in and occupy Baltimore until 1865.

Is this how the two Baltimores began? As a place split on ideologies because it's too south to be north and too north to be south–was this the start?

It is now 149 years later and nothing has changed. I went to all-black schools, lived in an all-black neighborhood, and had almost no interactions with whites other than teachers and housing police until college, where I got my first introduction to the other Baltimore.

Excerpt from D. Watkins,
"These are My Two Baltimores:
Black and White, The Beast Side"

You see how D. sees the city, but how do you see it? Are you from Baltimore, new to Baltimore, or just passing by?

Explain your Baltimore.

_____

_____

_____

_____

_____

_____

_____

_____

_____

_____

_____

_____

_____

White Man Walking

Tariq Touré

"The gentleman in this photo is in a period of transition in his life. Depending on his decisions, he'll experience a rock bottom that will forever alter his path. On the contrary, he is also tasked with choosing a healthy route. The healthy choice looks murky and is overwhelmingly covered with uncertainty and pain. It'll take blood. And the fresh blood is juxtaposed to what lies behind. Even though his past is drawing him backwards his body is facing the direction of the trial that will free him. He will win, but not before the old him dies."

Kondwani Fidel

"It shows the uniqueness and grittiness of city life with the alley ways and the marble steps. The guy looks like he could be coming from work doing maybe construction. When I first looked at him I said maybe he's homeless or a bum because of the way he dresses. But who am I to judge?"

D. Watkins

"Bull shit and bills in every direction. Left, right, left-right. Grannie said, "When you're lost baby, every direction is right.""

This book was designed to promote free thinking. Every image has its own narrative through different eyes. Create your own story using your imagination, exploring your hopes, or reliving your experiences. No two books will be exactly alike.

HOW TO USE THIS BOOK

Perspective: Baltimore

IMAGES BY: KYLE POMPEY

WRITTEN BY: _____

"The things you fear most
will be most helpful on your journey."

KYLE POMPEY

"FREE YOURSELF FROM

NEGATIVITY AND BE KING."

KYLE POMPEY

"WHEN I GROW,

WE GROW."

KYLE POMPEY

"The sun won't always shine on you. Just know there's always going to be trials and tribulations in life, but you have to keep being positive and believe in yourself."

KYLE POMPEY

"IT IS WHAT

YOU THINK IT IS."

KYLE POMPEY

"HOW CAN YOU LIVE YOUR LIFE

NEVER CHALLENGING YOURSELF?"

KYLE POMPEY

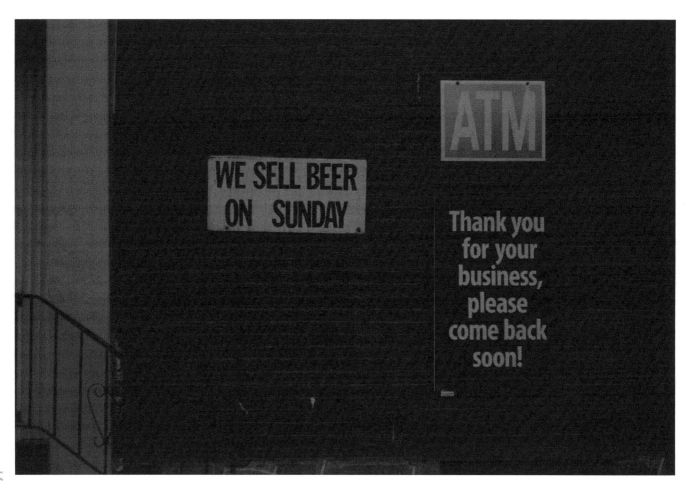

"Sometimes they gon'
have to hate you."

KYLE POMPEY

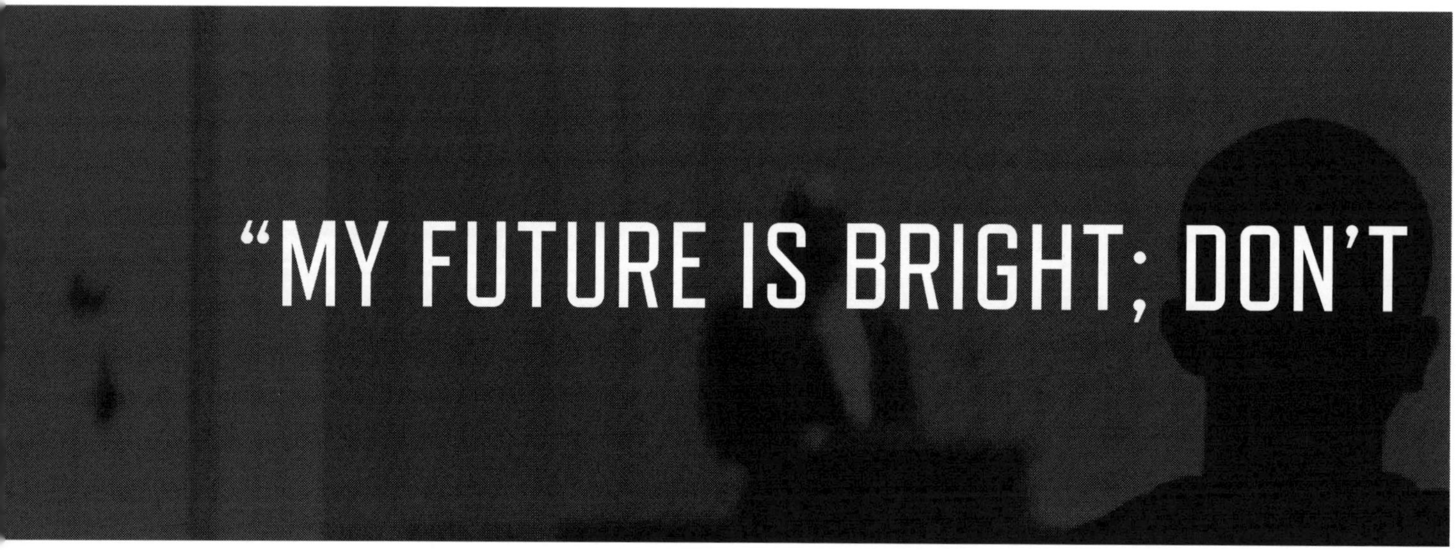
“MY FUTURE IS BRIGHT; DON’T

ASK ME ABOUT MY PAST."

KYLE POMPEY

"They program you to believe it's only one way to go and then they get scared when you figure out there's another."

KYLE POMPEY

_____

_____

_____

_____

_____

_____

_____

_____

_____

_____

_____

_____

_____

"Be exceptional
or humble, or both,
but anything in between
can be disastrous."

KYLE POMPEY

"Your gift can take
you places your character
can't keep you."

KYLE POMPEY

"ALWAYS HAVE SOMETHING

TO LOOK FORWARD TO."

KYLE POMPEY

Kyle Pompey

BLACK MAN

"Strong as a hybrid bull
our people on the streets far from full
but we are full of the bull... Shit!

Here comes another one--hand
out asking for another one.
If the shoe were on the other one
would you feel like you ever won?"

KYLE POMPEY

"GOTTA LIVE THROUGH IT TO KNOW

THAT YOU DON'T WANT TO GO BACK."

KYLE POMPEY

Freethought Space

ACKNOWLEDGEMENTS

Baltimore, Baltimore, oh how I love thee!

I would like to thank Kerry Graham for being an innovator, pushing her students, or her "lovelies," to be as great as they were born to be, and for not being afraid to try something new. A high school teacher who cares about her "lovelies" so much that she thought of ways to keep them interested in learning—not being a cookie-cutter teacher that most of us had growing up.

See, most curriculum is the same throughout public schools, but the children aren't. Every child has their own unique situation. They come from different neighborhoods, have different religions, and different issues that they deal with on a daily basis. How can you teach each individual child the same? I believe that the system is problematic in creating robots; Kerry recognized that and decided to challenge the free thought of her "lovelies" by using my images for their Socratic Seminars—building awareness of perspective. I sat in during one of the Socratic Seminars and was in awe of the different perspectives of my photos. That was the day Perspective: Baltimore was conceived. So for that, I thank you, Kerry. (Not to mention, she edited the book, too.)

I would like to thank Nikiea Redmond for designing the book. You did an awesome job. Your energy was amazing throughout the whole process and your patience was unbelievable.

I would like to thank D. Watkins for writing my preface from the heart. It means more than you know. You make me a proud pop every day. (Just kidding.)

I would also like to thank D. Watkins, along with Tariq Touré and Kondwani Fidel, for contributing your perspectives of "White Man Walking."

I would like to thank my proofreaders: Sadiq Ali, Tsonanda Edwards, Kevin Lei, and Lester Spence. I appreciate the time and effort you put into giving me feedback. You were a tremendous help.

I want to thank my family, starting with my mother, Alexis. You are one of my biggest supporters, motivators, morale boosters, G-checkers, and an all-around great woman. I love you, Ma! Thank you to my kids, Tyrin, Karmen, and Jordan: had it not been for you, I don't know what I would be doing with my life. I appreciate y'all keeping me honest and holding me accountable. Those things have shaped me to be the man I am today. Last but not least, I want to thank my wife, Keayra, who is my voice of reason, reality checker, picker-upper of all my missing pieces, and best friend. I love you.

Kyle Pompey considers himself an "organic photojournalist." Whether photographing in his studio, for a shoot, or in the street, Kyle avoids posed or planned pictures. Instead, he perceives the energy of his subject, which then guides the story Kyle captures in each moment. Baltimore born and raised, Kyle takes pictures of what he knows, and what feels like home to him. He notes that this means he photographs the sides of life, particularly in Baltimore, that people want to overlook. "People don't want to acknowledge it," Kyle says. "So nothing's happening. I use photography to stop time. I want to let people see what's going on through the pictures."

KYLEPOMPEY.COM

ABOUT THE AUTHOR & PHOTOGRAPHER

Share your favorite

freethought and use the hashtag

#PERSPECTIVEBALTIMORE